Remote Jungles

Stephanie Fitzgerald

Heinemann
LIBRARY

www.heinemann.co.uk/library
Visit our website to find out more information about Heinemann Library books.

To order:
 Phone 44 (0) 1865 888066
 Send a fax to 44 (0) 1865 314091
 Visit the Heinemann Bookshop at www.heinemann.co.uk/library to browse our catalogue and order online.

Produced for Heinemann Library by
White-Thomson Publishing Ltd,
Bridgewater Business Centre,
210 High Street,
Lewes, East Sussex BN7 2NH

First published in Great Britain by Heinemann Library,
Jordan Hill, Oxford OX2 8EJ, part of Harcourt
Education Ltd.

Consultant: Dr. Patrick Meir
Commissioning Editors: Sarah Shannon
  and Steve White-Thomson
Editor: Harriet Brown
Design: Tim Mayer
Artwork: William Donohoe
Production: Duncan Gilbert

Originated by Chroma Graphics (Overseas) Pte. Ltd.
Printed in China by South China Printing Co. Ltd.

ISBN 978-0-431-90742-0
12 11 10 09 08
10 9 8 7 6 5 4 3 2 1

British Library Cataloguing in Publication Data
Fitzgerald, Stephanie
Remote jungles. – (Earth's final frontiers)
333.7'5
A full catalogue record for this book is available from
the British Library.

Acknowledgements
The author and publisher would like to thank the
following for allowing their pictures to be reproduced in
this publication:

Alamy: 8–9 (Jon Arnold Images), 13 (Dave and Sigrun
Tollerton), 14 (blickwinkel), 22 (Jef Maion/Nomads'Land
– www.maion.com), 23 (Suzanne Long); Rob Bowden:
3, 6, 9, 25t, 27t, 29, 35, 41; Corbis: 10 (Frans Lemmens/
zefa), 15t (Theo Allofs), 17 (Frans Lanting), 18, 19, 20
(Hulton-Deutsch Collection), 28 (Colin McPherson),
37 (Collart Herve/Corbis Sygma); Getty images: 30
(James Balog); iStock: **title page** (Joe Gough), 15b, 16t
(Andreas Huber), 33, 38r (Howard Sandler); NASA Earth
Observatory: 32, 40; Oxford Scientific: 7 (Nordicphotos/
Chad Ehlers), 21 (Michael Fogden); Photolibrary: 16b
(Animals Animals/Earth Scenes/Joe McDonald), 26
(Robert Harding Picture Library Ltd/Bruno Barbier), 27b
(Phototake Inc/Bildagentur-online GmbH), 36 (Aurora
Photos/Gregg Adams); Laurent Pyot: 24, 25b, 31;
Steve White-Thomson: 11, 34, 38l, 39.

Cover photograph of Hawaii, Big Island, North Hilo
Stream, reproduced with permission of Pacific Stock
(Photolibrary).

Every effort has been made to contact copyright holders
of any material reproduced in this book. Any omissions
will be rectified in subsequent printings if notice is given
to the publishers.

CONTENTS

Words appearing in the text in bold, **like this**,
are explained in the glossary.

Tropic of Cancer

NORTH AMERICA

Venezuelan
rainforest

Colombian
rainforest

Brazilian
rainforest

Equator

Peruvian
rainforest

SOUTH AMERICA

Tropic of Capricorn

▼ *The jungles, or tropical rainforests, of Earth are found in the hot, steamy tropics. The tropics are the areas on or near the equator, between the tropic of Cancer and the tropic of Capricorn. These rainforests only cover about six percent of Earth's land surface, but they are home to more than half of the world's plant and animal species. These **diverse**, **remote** regions of Earth have attracted explorers for generations.*

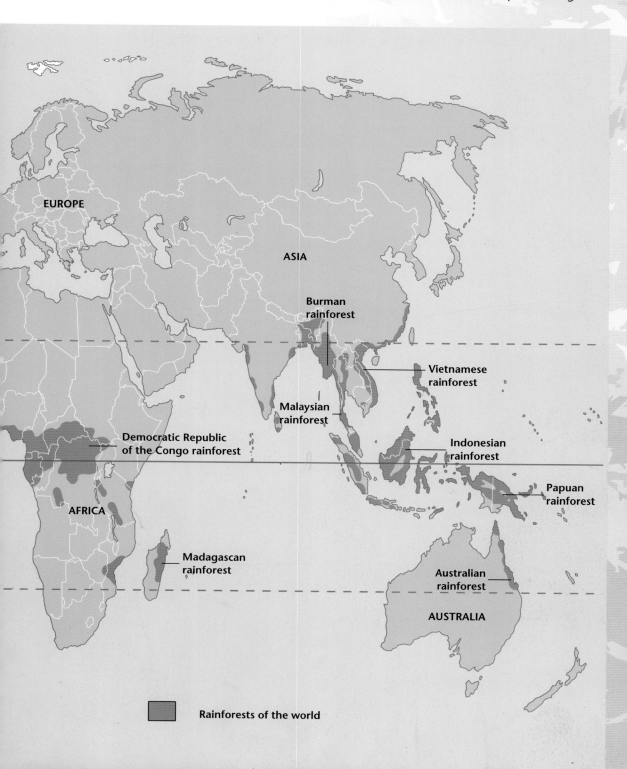

EUROPE

ASIA

Burman rainforest

Vietnamese rainforest

Malaysian rainforest

Democratic Republic of the Congo rainforest

Indonesian rainforest

Papuan rainforest

AFRICA

Madagascan rainforest

Australian rainforest

AUSTRALIA

Rainforests of the world

WHAT IS A FRONTIER?

For thousands of years humans have been exploring, discovering, and mapping Earth. We have even left Earth, and begun to explore outer space. Yet there are still some parts of Earth that remain little explored or understood.

EARTH'S FINAL FRONTIERS

The word frontier is often used to describe a remote place that is hard to reach and difficult to explore. But the word also refers to the farthest limit of knowledge that humankind has in a particular area of study. Both definitions apply to jungles.

When you think about jungles, you probably picture lush forests, brimming with colourful flowers, tall trees draped with vines, and **exotic** animals. When scientists use the word jungle, they are referring to tropical rainforests. This book will concentrate on remote tropical rainforests around the world.

GETTING THERE IS HALF THE JOB

When people first started exploring the rainforests, they faced many physical challenges. When an explorer came across a rainforest for the first time, he or she had no idea how big it might be, or what might be found inside. There were no trails to follow, so it was easy to get lost among the thousands of trees. But getting lost was not the only danger. Rainforests are literally crawling with insects, spiders, and snakes that can kill – swiftly and painfully – or carry diseases such as yellow fever.

▼ *The image most commonly associated with rainforests is a sea of green treetops stretching as far as the eye can see.*

TEMPERATE RAINFORESTS

Tropical rainforests are found around the world in areas near the equator. But there is another type of rainforest that grows in cooler regions. These are called **temperate** rainforests. Half of the temperate rainforests on Earth are found in the northwest of the United States. Other temperate rainforests can be found in northwest Europe, southeastern Australia, southern Chile, and on the west coast of New Zealand's South Island. Both tropical and temperate rainforests experience a large amount of rainfall during the year and contain **evergreen** trees.

A NEW FRONTIER

Modern technology has taken some of the mystery out of rainforest exploration. Satellite images tell us exactly where the world's rainforests are, and how large an area they cover. But knowing how big a rainforest is does not change the fact that people are exploring new areas all the time. New species of plants and animals are always being discovered, even today. In some rainforests, previously unknown tribes have even been discovered in recent years.

The world's rainforests play an important role in influencing **climate** locally, regionally, and globally. They are also being destroyed at an alarming rate. Many people are trying to discover just what effect this destruction will have on the world's climate. This represents a scientific and research frontier.

▲ Evergreen conifers dominate temperate rainforests, such as this one found on the Olympic Peninsula in Washington state, USA.

In their own words...

"I never beheld so fair a thing; trees beautiful and green and different from ours, with flowers and fruits each according to their kind, many and little birds, which sing very sweetly."
Christopher Columbus (1451–1506), on entering the rainforests of Haiti for the first time, in 1492.

EARTH'S GREEN FRONTIERS

Tropical rainforests are found near the equator, between the tropic of Cancer and the tropic of Capricorn. Because ice did not penetrate these equatorial regions completely during the last **ice age**, parts of these rainforests are millions of years old. Lowland rainforests occur near sea level. Rainforests that are found at higher **elevations** are called cloud forests and montane forests.

AFRICA

Rainforests are found in more than 15 African nations. The Democratic Republic of the Congo (DRC), in central Africa, contains the largest area of rainforest on the continent. In fact, the DRC contains one-tenth of the entire world's rainforest area. Parts of the mountain rainforests of eastern Africa are 40 million years old. Collectively, these rainforests are called the Eastern Arc because they are on a range of mountains that form a crescent shape. This area is famous for its incredible **biodiversity**. Biodiversity refers to the number of plant and animal species in a given area.

MADAGASCAR

Madagascar is an island that lies off the eastern coast of Africa. It features a very diverse collection of plants and animals, and is the only place on the planet where lemurs naturally live. In fact, of the 200,000 species of animal known to live on the island, 150,000 are **endemic**. This means they cannot be found naturally anywhere else in the world.

▼ *The mighty River Amazon snakes its way through the rainforest.*

▲ *Ferns and young trees are growing thickly in this east-African rainforest.*

SOUTHEAST ASIA

Southeast Asia is made up of a chain of about 20,000 islands that lie between Asia and Australia. Parts of the rainforests found here are the oldest on Earth. They formed 70–100 million years ago, when dinosaurs still roamed Earth. Unfortunately, this region is also losing its rainforests faster than any other on the planet.

CENTRAL AND SOUTH AMERICA

The area that connects North and South America is home to seven small countries. Guatemala, Belize, El Salvador, Honduras, Nicaragua, Costa Rica, and Panama all contain rainforests and, despite their small size, are rich in biodiversity. For example, the tiny country of Panama has more than 700 species of bird. That is more species than are found in all of North America!

South America is home to the most famous and largest rainforest on Earth: the Amazon. There are more species of plants and animals living in the Amazon than anywhere else on Earth. It is estimated that 30 percent of the world's species can be found there.

A massive river runs through the Amazon. The River Amazon is the largest in the world, discharging up to 14 billion cubic metres (cu m) (500 billion cubic feet [cu ft]) of water into the Atlantic Ocean every day. In fact, about one-fifth of all the fresh water running into the world's oceans flows out of the Amazon.

AUSTRALIA

The driest inhabited continent on Earth, Australia would not seem to be a likely place for a rainforest. But at the northeastern part of Queensland lies an area known as the "Wet Tropics". Although this area only covers one percent of Australia's total land mass, it is home to a huge variety of plant and animal species.

WHAT MAKES A TROPICAL RAINFOREST?

Not every tropical rainforest is exactly the same, but they all share certain characteristics. To be considered a tropical rainforest, an area must receive more than 2 metres (m) (6.5 feet [ft]) of rainfall per year. The forest must also stay pretty warm, between 21 degrees Celsius (°C) and 29°C (70 degrees Fahrenheit [°F] and 85°F), without a lot of change in temperature from day to day. Because of this, rainforests do not have traditional seasons – spring, summer, winter, and autumn. Instead, seasons here are considered "dry" or "wet".

Rainforests contain a high level of biodiversity. There are also likely to be **symbiotic** relationships between species. A symbiotic relationship is where individuals of one species provide those of another with resources, such as food or help with reproduction, and vice versa. In this way, both sets of individuals benefit. For example, a bird might eat the fruit from a certain tree. Then the bird passes the fruit seeds in its droppings, and more trees grow. Both the tree and the bird are benefiting from their relationship.

WATER WORLD

Rainforests are often located in **river basins** near some of the largest rivers in the world. A river basin is the land that surrounds a river. River basins are often shaped like saucers. All the water that collects on the land drains into the river.

▼ Local people call Victoria Falls in eastern Africa "Mosi-oa-Tunya", "the smoke that thunders". On average, 550,000 cu m (19.4 million cu ft) of water cascade over the edge of the falls every minute.

Many rainforest rivers grow so large because huge amounts of rain falls and collects in the basin, and eventually runs down to the river. These rivers are also fed by smaller streams and rivers, called **tributaries**, which flow into the main river. Rainforests also often contain waterfalls and **oxbow** lakes.

River water flows fastest on the outside edge of a river bend. As it flows, it erodes the outer edge of the riverbank. A river flows more slowly on the inside of a bend, so it deposits mud and sand there as it moves. Over time, this erosion and depositing of materials creates an oxbow lake.

▼ *As the outside of a river bend is eroded, the water flow moves further from the river's original course. The material that is deposited on the inside bends of the river eventually cuts this new section of water off from the rest of the river, creating an oxbow lake.*

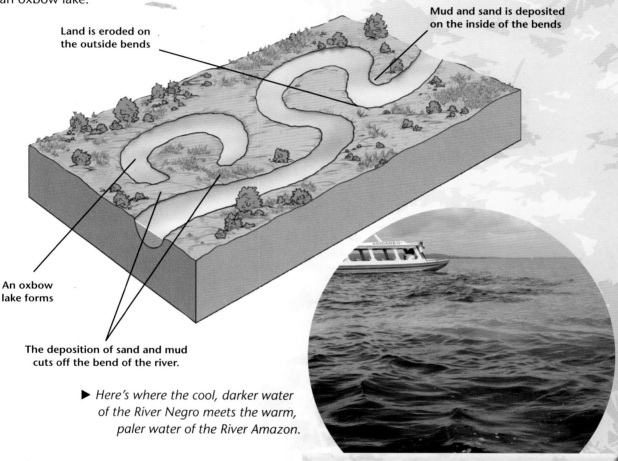

Land is eroded on the outside bends

Mud and sand is deposited on the inside of the bends

An oxbow lake forms

The deposition of sand and mud cuts off the bend of the river.

▶ *Here's where the cool, darker water of the River Negro meets the warm, paler water of the River Amazon.*

ROCKS AND MINERALS

The rock and **mineral** content of the land beneath rainforests varies. Rainforests in parts of Venezuela, West Africa, Australia, and Brazil contain exposed rock that is very old. Some of it dates back 600 million years. This rock is rich in gold, diamonds, iron, and bauxite (which contains aluminium). Rock in rainforests in other parts of the world, such as Nigeria, is rich in oil deposits.

A RIVER OF TEA

The River Negro, which means Black River, gets its name from the colour of its waters. Though the water looks black from above, it is actually the colour of tea. The brown water is not caused by **pollution** – it is caused by the **vegetation** that falls into the river from nearby trees.

LIFE IN THE FOREST

When you picture a rainforest, you probably think of a vast, unbroken "carpet" of treetops. But rainforests actually have different layers. The layer of treetops seen from an aircraft is the **upper canopy**. It is located 20–45 m (65–150 ft) off the ground. Beneath the upper canopy are the **understorey** and then the forest floor.

THE UPPER CANOPY

This is the layer of rainforest that receives the most sunlight. It is home to 90 percent of the named **organisms** found in any rainforest, making it one of the most diverse **habitats** on Earth.

The branches of these gigantic canopy trees are often covered with **epiphytes**. Epiphytes are plants that grow on other plants, such as trees, but do not take any **nutrients** from their host. They include colourful orchids and bromeliads, another flowering plant. Since they live near the treetops, they need to be clever in getting water. Some epiphytes have leaves that form bowls to catch rainwater.

Lianas also live among the branches of upper canopy trees. Lianas are woody vines that grow on the branches of the trees and across the treetops. The vines act like a road in the sky, linking the tops of the trees, and creating a way for animals to travel from one tree to another.

THE UNDERSTOREY

This area of the forest is dark and not very populated. Because the upper canopy layer is so dense, little sunlight makes it through the tangle of leaves to the forest below. The understorey usually receives less than five percent of the sunlight that shines on the forest. **Saplings** of canopy trees can be found here, as well as shrubs and plants that do not need a lot of light.

Because of the low-light conditions, the understorey is often relatively clear. Most plants cannot grow well in low-light conditions. The understorey only becomes overgrown along rivers and roadways, or where a canopy tree has fallen. These are the areas where sunlight is able to reach the ground.

▼ *This diagram shows the main layers found in a tropical rainforest.*

Emergents

Upper canopy

Understorey

Forest floor

THE RAINFOREST FLOOR

The rainforest floor hardly sees any sunlight at all. Not many plants grow here, but the floor is still crawling with life. It is covered with a thin layer of fallen leaves, fruit, seeds, and dead branches that quickly **decompose** with the help of **microbes**, fungi, and insects.

Most of the nutrients in a rainforest are found in the vegetation. What nutrients are found in rainforest soil are mainly found in the upper layers of the soil. Rainforest trees have adapted by growing some of their roots along the forest floor. The network of interlacing roots that results is called a root mat. Some giant canopy trees have deep roots that are used to get water during dry periods. Some huge trees can also develop buttress roots. Experts think these extra-thick roots stop the trees from falling over in unstable soil.

PHOTOSYNTHESIS

The upper canopy is where most **photosynthesis** occurs in the rainforest. During photosynthesis, the leaves of the upper canopy trees soak up sunlight and make their own food. In this process they take in carbon dioxide and release oxygen into the air.

▼ *Buttress roots provide support for the massive upper canopy trees.*

WEIRD AND WILD

Thanks to the incredible diversity of plant life found there, Earth's rainforests are also home to an amazing variety of animals. Many of these animals can only be found in their rainforest homes. Others look like gigantic versions of animals and insects found elsewhere.

THE BIGGEST AND BADDEST

The rainforests are home to a wide variety of spiders, including several types of tarantula – some that grow to the size of a dinner plate! Right now, the goliath tarantula (*Theraphosa blondi*) holds the record as the largest spider on Earth. This monster, which is found in the rainforests of Venezuela, can grow up to 28 centimetres (cm) (11 inches [in]) across. The goliath is also known as the bird-eater, because it likes to pull little birds from their nests and devour them. It also eats frogs, small snakes, lizards, beetles, and bats.

The goliath spider might sound big, but researchers think that they might have found an even larger tarantula in the Tambopata Reserve at the western edge of the Amazon basin in Peru. At the moment, scientists are calling this tarantula the chicken spider – and not because it's afraid of other spiders. Witnesses claim to have seen one of these spiders dragging a chicken into its den.

HAIR-RAISING DEFENCE

When threatened, a goliath tarantula will make a hissing noise by rubbing its legs together. The noise is so loud, it can be heard up to 4.5 m (15 ft) away. The goliath can also defend itself by shooting the tiny hairs on its body at any creature it sees as a threat.

▼ *The goliath spider, which measures almost 28 cm (11 in) across, is currently the largest confirmed tarantula on Earth.*

LOUD AND PROUD

Howler monkeys are the loudest land animals on Earth, and can be heard up to 4.8 kilometres (km) (3 miles) away. The largest of the New World monkeys, this **primate** lives in the rainforest canopies of southern Brazil, northern Argentina, Paraguay, and Bolivia.

Marching wasps are another noisy bunch. When these insects hear a loud, threatening noise, the entire group starts to beat their wings in unison. The sound of this "marching" is intended to scare off potential **predators**.

▲ *Howler monkeys live in groups called troops. Howlers use their loud voices to defend the troop's territory.*

DANGEROUS ANIMALS

Bullet ants are among the world's most **venomous** insects, and the rainforests are just crawling with them! They are called bullet ants because their bite feels like a bullet wound. These ants can grow to 2.5 cm (1 in) long, and they make a warning noise when threatened.

Boa constrictors are snakes found in the rainforests of Central and South America. They are not venomous – instead they squeeze their prey to death. These huge snakes can grow up to 4 m (13 ft) in length.

▶ *Boa constrictors are nocturnal (night) hunters. They hang from trees at cave entrances, and snatch bats out of the air. They squeeze the breath from the bats, and swallow them whole.*

ONE OF A KIND

Many animals are endemic to the rainforests where they live. This means that they do not occur naturally anywhere else on Earth. Of course, many of these creatures can often be found far from their traditional homes in zoos around the world.

ANIMALS OF THE AMERICAS

Colourful frogs are some of the animals most commonly associated with rainforests. As with any animal, their bright colours often serve as a warning. Poison arrow frogs, found in Central and South America, are actually **toxic**. Local hunters use the frogs' poison on the tips of their arrows and blowpipe darts.

▲ *Red-eyed tree frogs have suction disks on their toes and fingers that help them stick to tree leaves.*

▼ *Basilisk lizards can run across water for 4.5 m (15 ft) before they drop to all fours and swim. They do this by generating forces with their feet. If they stop running they sink.*

Central and South American rainforests are also home to the sloth. This mammal spends most of its life hanging upside down from the upper canopy. Sloths rarely turn right side up. In fact, they eat, sleep, mate, and even give birth hanging upside down!

The basilisk is a lizard that lives in the rainforests of South America. What makes this creature so unusual is its ability to run across the surface of water. The basilisk runs on its back legs, holding its body upright, with its tail acting as a counterbalance.

▲ *The smelly rafflesia plant can only be found in Indonesia.*

STINK BUD

Rainforests are also home to some unusual plants. The rafflesia plant (*Rafflesia arnoldii*), found in Indonesia, has the largest flower in the world. It grows up to 1 m (3 ft) in diameter. More unusual than the flower's size, though, is the way it smells – like rotting meat. Scientists think the flower uses this smell to attract meat-eating insects that help with **pollination**.

ADAPTED TO AUSTRALIA AND ASIA

The frilled-neck lizard is a rare lizard that lives in New Guinea and northern Australia. It has a brightly coloured flap of skin, or frill, 18–34 cm (7–14 in) wide that completely encircles its head. The lizard opens this frill to scare off predators. Like the basilisk, this lizard can run on four legs or two.

Orang-utans are only found on the Indonesian islands of Sumatra and Borneo. They are the only strictly **arboreal** apes in the world. This means that orang-utans spend all of their time in the trees.

ANIMALS OF AFRICA

The bonobo (*Pan paniscus*), which can only be found in the rainforests of the Democratic Republic of the Congo, was the last species of great ape ever discovered. This peaceful creature is the most human-like in the animal world. Bonobos and humans share 98.4 percent of the same DNA.

The okapi (*Okapia johnstoni*) is an unusual creature that is found only in the rainforest of the upper Congo river basin. This animal, also known as the forest giraffe, is rarely seen and was only discovered in the 20th century. The bongo (*Tragelaphus eurycerus*) is a rare antelope that also lives in the rainforests of Africa. Its brown coat with white stripes helps it blend into its forest habitat.

EARLY EXPLORATION

People were living in the world's rainforests for thousands of years before these areas were "discovered" by Europeans. But by the 18th century, Europeans were expanding their **influence** around the globe. Travel was hard, but explorers were anxious to discover new lands. They wanted to find new natural resources, such as food products, medicinal plants, rubber, hardwoods for building, and valuable minerals, such as gold.

EQUATOR EXPERIMENTS

In the early 18th century, there was some debate about whether Earth was wider around the equator or around the Poles. In 1735, the king of France sent Charles Marie de la Condamine (1701–74) to make measurements at the equator. To accomplish this, Condamine travelled to Colombia, Panama, and Ecuador, and explored the Amazon rainforest.

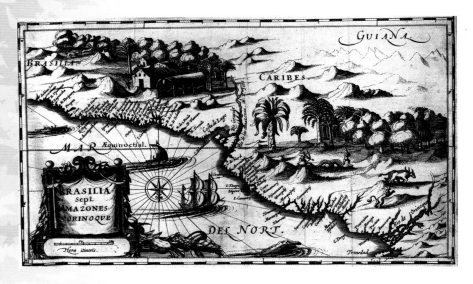

Condamine's equator experiments ended in 1739, but he remained in South America for four more years. He spent his time rafting down the River Amazon, collecting **specimens**, and mapping the mighty river. He also studied the local population. He found it confusing that they feasted when food was abundant, and starved when it was scarce. He did not understand why they didn't save food for hard times, but of course it was impossible to preserve food in the hot, tropical environment. The local population knew that it was best to eat food while it was fresh.

▲ More than 300 years ago, when this map was drawn, Europeans knew very little about what lay beyond the coastline of South America. It wasn't until the 18th century that explorers ventured further into the continent. The map is actually "upside down" so the bottom of the map represents north.

HUMBOLDT IN SOUTH AMERICA

The first European to more fully explore the rainforests of Central and South America was Baron Alexander von Humboldt (1769–1859). Humboldt was a Prussian **naturalist** and explorer who travelled with botanist Aime-Jacques-Alexandre Goujoud Bonpland (1773–1858). Between 1799 and 1805, they explored Mexico, Colombia, Ecuador, Peru, the coast of Venezuela, and the Amazon and Orinoco rivers.

During these trips, they collected many plant and animal specimens, and made contact with several native tribes. Humboldt was also a **conservationist**. At the time, the cinchona plant, which is used to make quinine – a treatment for malaria – was being over-harvested. Humboldt was the first person to recommend that cinchona should be preserved.

BATES, WALLACE, AND SPRUCE

In 1848, British naturalists, Henry Walter Bates (1825–92) and Alfred Russel Wallace (1823–1913), travelled to the River Amazon basin to study insects. Wallace stayed for 4 years, but Bates stayed for 11. During that time, Bates collected hundreds of specimens that he sent to museums and collectors in Europe.

In 1849, another British naturalist landed in South America. Richard Spruce (1817–93) spent 15 years travelling throughout Brazil, Peru, Ecuador, and Venezuela, where he collected many plant specimens. Spruce was one of the explorers responsible for collecting cinchona seeds. By planting these seeds, the British government produced quinine in their colonies, saving many people from malaria. While in South America, Spruce worked very closely with the **indigenous** people. He learned the languages of 21 tribes, and gained knowledge of how they used rainforest plants to treat illness.

▲ *Wallace's writings about his travels to the Amazon and Southeast Asia were said to have inspired naturalist Charles Darwin's work. Charles Darwin developed important theories about natural selection and **evolution** (how species change gradually over very long periods of time).*

LIVINGSTONE IN AFRICA

David Livingstone (1813–73) was a famous British explorer who went to Africa as a **missionary**. Livingstone's primary reason for going to Africa in 1841 was to convert the natives to Christianity. However, he also spent more than 20 years exploring the continent. While searching for the source of the River Nile, Livingstone became the first European to see the spectacular Victoria Falls (see page 10).

KINGSLEY EXPLORES AFRICA

In 1893, British explorer, Mary Henrietta Kingsley (1862–1900), ignored the conventional ideas of her time by travelling to West and Central Africa. In the 19th century, the very idea of a woman travelling alone was virtually unheard of.

For her first trip to West Africa, Kingsley planned to study religion and write about her adventures. She travelled along the coast of West Africa for several months before heading inland. She explored the River Congo, collecting many scientific specimens for the British Museum.

On her second trip to West Africa, Kingsley became the first European to visit the rainforests of the French Congo (today, this area is made up of the Republic of the Congo, Gabon, Chad, and the Central African Republic). During her travels, Kingsley spent time with the Fang tribe, who were well known as fierce **cannibals**.

When she returned home from her travels, Kingsley wrote a book called *Travels in West Africa*. The book showed sympathy for African natives and criticized European interference on the continent. Kingsley wanted to ensure that Africans remained free, and not enslaved by Europeans. The book was not very popular at the time.

▲ *David Livingstone spent more time exploring Africa than anyone ever had before. In fact, he was gone so long that newspapers reported him dead.*

▲ *Alfred Wallace discovered the gliding tree frog while exploring the tropical rainforests of Southeast Asia.*

SURVEYING SOUTHEAST ASIA

Two years after returning from the Amazon rainforest, Alfred Russel Wallace travelled to Malaysia and Indonesia. Between 1854 and 1862, he studied the **ecology** of the rainforests in this region and collected specimens, most notably the gliding tree frog, which was eventually called Wallace's flying frog.

During his explorations, Wallace noticed that there seemed to be a difference between animal species found in the region closer to Asia and those found nearer Australia. The observation of this boundary helped him to develop ideas about natural selection similar to those developed by Charles Darwin (1809–82). The boundary runs between the islands of Borneo and Sulawesi, and between the islands of Bali and Lombok. It was later named the Wallace Line.

RAINFOREST EXPLORATION

1735: Charles Maria de la Condamine travels to South America.

1799–1805: Baron Alexander von Humboldt and Aime-Jacques-Alexandre Goujoud Bonpland explore the Amazon.

1848–52: Alfred Russel Wallace explores the Amazon.

1848–59: Henry Walter Bates explores the Amazon.

1849–64: Richard Spruce explores Brazil, Peru, Ecuador, and Venezuela.

1853: David Livingstone arrives in Africa.

1854–62: Wallace explores Malaysia and Indonesia.

1860: Dr. Livingstone becomes the first European to see Victoria Falls.

1893: Mary Henrietta Kingsley arrives in West Africa.

CROSSING THE FINAL FRONTIER

Thanks to satellite images and early explorers, we know where all the rainforests in the world can be found. But there are still parts of these rainforests that remain unexplored – and thousands of plants and animals that are new to science. Although explorers do not need to hack their way through the rainforest as actors do in films, there are still very real **obstacles** to rainforest exploration.

GETTING THERE

When people want to explore **isolated** areas of a rainforest, they are often travelling where no one has before. This means that there are no roads or trails to follow. For some expeditions, explorers have to be brought in by small aeroplanes or helicopters. Even in areas that have been explored, people still have to drive for hours over muddy, bumpy roads. Once they are dropped off, they have to hike into the forest to their campsites carrying everything they need on their backs – clothes, food, and even heavy research equipment!

Reaching the campsite can also be dangerous. Anyone exploring the rainforest knows that you always have to watch where you walk, and where you place your hands. Some shrubs are armed with sharp spines or stinging hairs. Tree trunks could be crawling with biting ants. And the forest floor is alive with snakes and spiders, not to mention larger predators such as jaguars.

▼ *Camping in a tropical rainforest can be a wet and wild experience.*

▲ Travelling through the rainforest is tough going. This explorer is using a rope to descend into the crater of the Maderas Volcano in Nicaragua.

In their own words...

"I love it here, but I can take it for ten days, maybe two weeks, and then I have to get out and get CLEANED UP! Before too long I'm dirty, my clothes smell, heck, I smell ... [But] it's really sort of liberating to be here. I can wear the same shirt for a week, I can look terrible, but it doesn't matter because I'm doing my work. "
Emilio Bruna (born 1972), a scientific researcher working in the Amazon rainforest.

DANGEROUS TREES

Another threat comes from the trees themselves. Giant, broken tree branches get tangled up in vines, and hang overhead. If someone trips over the wrong vine, they could dislodge a hanging branch, and send it crashing down on their head.

DIRTY WORK

The heat and **humidity** in a rainforest can even make sitting still seem like a lot of work! Temperatures can reach 34°C (93°F) with a humidity level of 88 percent. People who spend all day hiking through the forest can lose more than a kilogram (2.2 pounds) a day, just by sweating. That is why it is so important that people exploring the rainforest bring plenty of water to drink.

Rainforest camps are typically pretty primitive. Some explorers sleep in hammocks stretched between tree branches. They might bathe in a stream, and even wash their clothes there.

UNCHARTED TERRITORY

People who explore the rainforests often come from other areas. This can make it harder for them to identify certain plants and animals, find what they are looking for, and relate to the local people whose land they are visiting. Most researchers spend years studying an area they hope to explore, learning local languages and customs. They also work with people who are native to the area on their expeditions. Many scientists working in the Amazon rainforest work with a *mateiro*, which means "man of the forest". *Mateiros* are local people who act as guides, and usually know local names for the different tree species.

THE NEW FRONTIERS

For many years after explorers made their way into the depths of the rainforests, the upper canopy remained unexplored. Even though explorers have now developed ways to climb the giant trees, and move among their branches, this area of the rainforest is still called "the high frontier".

UNLOCKING THE MYSTERIES OF THE UPPER CANOPY

When researchers began exploring the upper canopy in the 1970s, the first obstacle was finding a way to get into the treetops and stay safe so high above the forest floor. At the time, researchers used the same kind of spikes to climb trees that telephone pole climbers used. No one really knew of a better way to climb the trees. Unfortunately, they did not realize that they were harming the very trees they hoped to study. The spikes made holes in the tree bark, which left an opening for disease or fungus to infect the tree.

Sometimes, researchers were also harming the organisms that were found on the tree trunks and branches. They did not realize that as they moved around, they were disturbing mosses or dead organic matter that had taken decades and decades to gather.

WHO'S WHO

Nalini Nadkarni (born 1954) has been called "the queen of forest canopy research". A true pioneer, Dr. Nadkarni is co-founder of the International Canopy Network. Her research is focused on the ecology of rainforest canopies, particularly the role that upper-canopy-dwelling plants play in the **ecosystem**. She conducts field research in the temperate rainforests of Washington state, USA, and the tropical rainforests of Monteverde, Costa Rica.

▼ *The balloon on the right is a canopy bubble. A researcher sits on a bench beneath the balloon. The small airship on the left is a dirigible that delivers researchers to the canopy raft.*

ON THE RIGHT TRACK

By the early 1980s, researchers were finding new ways to reach the upper canopy. The use of construction cranes was a big breakthrough. Researchers also began using mountain climbing techniques to reach the treetops.

In the 1990s, the canopy bubble was developed to help explore the upper reaches of the rainforest. The bubble is a hot air balloon that is hooked up to a little bench. A pilot runs the hot air balloon, and the researcher sits on the bench and is carried over the tree tops. The canopy bubble takes off wherever it can get through the upper canopy layer, and then it floats above the tree tops.

People have also built towers and walkways through the upper canopy in various places in the world. These walkways are used by scientists who are studying plants, animals, and insects, and they are even used by tourists.

▲ Walkways allow access to the upper canopy, but they do not allow people to study the very tops of the trees. Also, walkways are fixed, which limits how much of the upper canopy people can explore.

CANOPY RAFTS

However, there is only one way to truly explore the very top of the upper canopy. That is with the canopy raft. The raft is a series of inflatable hoops with a net spread in between. A small airship (**dirigible**) carries the raft to the tops of the trees and lays it right on the crowns – very tops – of the trees. People can then climb up to the raft or be lowered down on to it, and walk around on the actual top of the upper canopy, which is not really accessible using mountain climbing techniques.

▼ This airship is delivering researchers to the massive canopy raft. The canopy raft offers researchers the chance to walk over the very tops of rainforest trees.

SCIENTIFIC FRONTIERS

Researchers are working to discover how the rainforest ecosystem influences climate, how the plants and animals work together in this ecosystem, how to study the rainforests effectively, and more. Because rainforests cover huge tracts of land, new species of plants and animals are always being discovered.

HIDDEN MYSTERIES

Although rainforests cover just 6 percent of Earth's surface, it is believed that they contain more than 50 percent of all living things on the planet. More than 400,000 plant species have been identified in the Amazon rainforest alone. There are more ant species on one tree in the Amazon than in the entire United Kingdom.

In their own words...

"The sad reality is that many of these plants, including those that may contain cures to some of the world's most deadly diseases, may become extinct before they have even been discovered."
Olo Gebia, WWF Forest Ecologist.

Because many rainforests are so vast, it will take years before they can be explored completely. There are areas where no one has ever walked. At any given time, somewhere around the world, someone is walking over ground that no human has ever trodden on before.

▼ *The sheer size of rainforests means that there are areas that still contain unknown species of plants and animals.*

WILD KINGDOM

Scientists do not give an exact number for how many different animal species might live in the rainforests of the world. However, some estimate that it could be as many as 30 million. The estimate is so high because researchers are discovering new species all the time.

In December 2005, Conservation International led a team of scientists on an expedition to the rainforests of New Guinea's Foja Mountains. During that one-month trip, the group discovered more than 20 new frog species, and 4 new butterfly species. They also discovered a new species of honeyeater. This was the first new bird to be discovered in New Guinea since 1939. New species are being found in other rainforests, too. More than 350 new species have been found in Borneo since 1994. And during an expedition to the Rubeho Mountains in Tanzania, Africa, scientists discovered 11 new species.

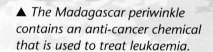

▲ The Madagascar periwinkle contains an anti-cancer chemical that is used to treat leukaemia.

NATURAL HEALING

Many rainforest plants are important for the health benefits they provide. At least 25 percent of the prescription drugs sold today originated in the rainforest. Probably the best-known drug that comes from the rainforest is quinine. This chemical, which comes from the cinchona plant, has been used to treat malaria since the 18th century. Curare, ipecac, wild yam, and Madagascar periwinkle are other examples of rainforest plants whose compounds have been used to fight major diseases such as cancer and heart disease.

▶ The bark of the cinchona tree contains quinine and can be made into a tea to help fight malaria.

FOREST PEOPLE

Five hundred years ago, there were approximately 10 million indigenous people living in the Amazon rainforest. Today there are fewer than 200,000. Indigenous people have moved from the rainforests to the cities. Sometimes city life offers more opportunities than life in the rainforest. However, there are many tribes still holding on to their traditional ways of life deep among the trees.

VILLAGES IN THE FOREST

In 2001, an expedition team from the Brazilian Government's Federal Indian Bureau met with members of the Tsohon-djapa tribe from a remote area of the Amazon. It was the first time that the tribe had ever had contact with members of western society. Members of the tribe knew about the existence of white people, but had never met any before. The Brazilian government discovered the tribe only after an aerial survey of the area showed a village containing 16 houses.

▼ *Rainforest people harvest the products of the rainforest for their own use and for trade.*

There have been many other discoveries of unknown tribes. A few years earlier, in 1998, Sydney Possuelo (born 1940), who leads Brazil's Department of Isolated Indians, came into contact with the Korubo tribe. The Korubo have a village deep in the Amazon rainforest. Making first contact with indigenous people can be dangerous. That is why explorers like Possuelo have to be very knowledgeable. Possuelo has led hundreds of expeditions into the Amazon rainforest and was familiar with the Korubo belief that only enemies arrive in silence. He and his team stood at the edge of the village singing until they were allowed to enter in peace.

PROTECTING TRIBES

Possuelo did not only want to study and befriend the tribespeople, he also wanted to protect them. Like many indigenous people of the rainforest, the Korubo were under threat from outsiders who wanted to take their land. These people, who wanted to cut down the trees or use the land for farming (see pages 32–33), often brought violence and disease with them. Possuelo and Brazil's Department of Isolated Indians work to protect tribal lands.

Like the Korubo, many rainforest tribes are under threat from outsiders – they are even under threat from people who want to help them. Most rainforest people are hunter-gatherers. They live off the plants and animals found in their forest homes. Some governments in countries with rainforests think it would be better for indigenous people to give up their traditional ways of life to become modernized. People like Sydney Possuelo are fighting to help tribal people keep their way of life.

MAKING A LIVING

Many rainforest dwellers are hunter-gatherers. They live off food provided by the forest, such as animals, fruit, and nuts. Today, some members of Amazonian tribes also earn money by collecting exotic fish for the aquarium market.

EXPLORING THE RAINFORESTS TODAY

Now that the physical barriers to exploring the rainforests have mostly been resolved, these regions have become a top destination for a new type of explorer. Today, scientific researchers and even tourists flock to the rainforests.

NATURALISTS AT WORK

Many scientists who explore the rainforest today focus on small parts of the forest, and study how they relate to the whole. For example, a scientist may study the droppings of howler monkeys to determine how seeds are spread throughout the forest. Another researcher might focus on epiphytes, and how these plants interact with a host tree, and with the animals that use them for food and shelter. Other scientists are dedicated to finding out how the rainforest helps influence the world's climate.

No matter what their particular area of study, though, all scientists have the same ultimate goal. That is to understand, protect, and **conserve** the forests and all the organisms living there.

▼ *The number of tigers in the wild has steadily declined due to loss of habitat.*

TRADITIONAL TECHNIQUES

Researchers used to rely on traditional techniques to study tigers. This involved looking for and identifying individual paw prints (or pugmarks) and actually capturing the animals, and fitting them with radio collars. Both of these techniques are hard to use in the rainforest because paw prints disappear quickly on the forest floor, and the dense upper canopy makes it hard to get a clear radio signal on the tracking collars. Today, camera traps help find the tigers (see page 31).

TOOLS OF THE TRADE

Studying the plants and animals found in the rainforest requires a lot of job-specific tools. For example, upper canopy researchers use cranes, mountain climbing equipment, and hot air balloons to reach their study sites.

Researchers who are studying animals have a bit of a challenge on their hands because animals move and hide, or worse still are only active at night! Often they need to capture the animals in order to measure, evaluate, and tag them. Naturalists who study birds and bats often use mist nets to capture specimens. These are lightweight, nearly invisible nets that can be used on the ground or strung between branches in the canopy. Once the nets are in place, the birds or bats fly into them and become trapped.

Scientists who study insects often use a fogger to capture their subjects. The fogger shoots out a **biodegradable** pesticide into the trees. The researcher then collects the insects that fall to the ground. Scientists also take measurements of insect sounds, which they can analyse on a computer to try to determine the level of biodiversity in the forests.

▲ This researcher is using a fogger. The fabric at the top of the image collects the insects killed by the pesticide, which can then be studied by the researcher.

CAMERA TRAPS

For some researchers, simply finding the animal they want to study is half the job. That is the case with tigers in the rainforests of India and Malaysia. There are so few tigers left that researchers have a hard time spotting them – not to mention studying them. Camera traps are these naturalists' secret weapon. The cameras, which are set off by animals passing in front of **infrared** sensors, are set up in areas where researchers think the animals roam. When a tiger trips one of the sensors as it passes by, the camera takes a picture. This technology is also being used to study jaguars in South American rainforests.

HIGH-TECH TOOLS IN A LOW-TECH WORLD

Advances in technology have made rainforest exploration and research easier. But because many rainforests are so widespread and the upper canopy is so high, it has been difficult to accurately describe the different tree species found there. Researchers had to walk through the forest identifying each tree individually. Now, scientists at the Geo Information Systems Laboratory (GISLAB) of the National Institute for Amazonian Research (INPA), Brazil, have developed a way to make that process easier. The GISLAB remote sensing project "teaches" a computer to recognize the different tree crowns shown in pictures taken by low-flying aircraft.

At the moment, because the technology is so new, this remote sensing requires checking by "ground truthing". This means that a researcher will go into a part of the forest that has been mapped by the GISLAB, and check the identity and size of the tree species by physically identifying the tree. Once the GISLAB system has been shown to work accurately, the ground-truthing step of the process can be phased out.

▼ Satellite images show rainforest areas in great detail. In this image, you can see which areas are forested, and which have been built upon. It also clearly shows that the water of the River Negro is much darker than the water of the River Amazon.

River Nègro

River Amazon

Mixing

ENCROACHMENT

Technology is also helping Amazon natives protect their land, which has been **encroached** upon in the past by various people. Commercial farmers have cleared trees to create farmland in remote patches of forest. Logging companies have come in to harvest valuable hardwood trees such as mahogany and teak. And mining companies have come in looking for gold and other precious minerals.

In the past, it had been nearly impossible to stop these people. The rainforests are so large that their activities would often go unnoticed. The local tribespeople did not even realize others were using their land. It was easy to hide a small airstrip among so many trees. Miners looking for gold would use sluice boxes to filter the gold from the river. A small sluice box on the bank of a river could easily go undetected. The locals also had a hard time fighting the encroachment because they could not prove that the land belonged to them.

PROTECTING THE LAND

Now, thanks to the Amazon Conservation Team (ACT), Amazon tribes have a way to protect their land. ACT is training members of the tribes in how to use Global Positioning Systems (GPS) and the Internet to map and catalogue the forest. By viewing pictures of their forest, the tribespeople can see disturbances that they might not have noticed before. Areas where trees have been cut down can be easily seen. Discolouration in a river can be the result of pollution or sedimentation caused by a gold mine. This disturbance can be spotted, its location is mapped, and the activity can be reported to government officials.

Mapping the forest also allows the tribes to establish their land rights. They can then appeal to conservation groups and their governments to help protect their homeland.

RAINFOREST CULTURE

The ACT project is also helping indigenous people in the Amazon preserve their culture. Many young people were leaving the forest to move to the cities. The ways of their elders were being forgotten. Learning this new technology has encouraged the young people to stay in their villages. It has also encouraged them to learn the traditions and ways of their elders, who help the youngsters locate different landmarks in the forest.

▼ *Logging companies take down trees in a large area of forest. They sell the wood to be made into furniture.*

ECOTOURISM

Other people who explore the rainforests come armed only with a camera. Some rainforests have become popular holiday destinations for people who are interested in conservation, wildlife, and adventure travel. These visitors can stroll among the canopy on walkways in the sky, raft the massive rainforest rivers, and hike the forest floor looking for exotic wildlife.

As long as these holiday tours are run responsibly, so that tourists do not harm the ecosystem they are visiting, **ecotourism** can benefit the world's rainforests. The more people know about these regions, the more interested they will be in conserving them. If the local government and local people can make money by running ecotours, they might be less likely to destroy the rainforest for profit, by selling timber, **poaching** animals, or using the land for farming.

PROFITING FROM LOSS

Unlike naturalists and ecotourists, some people who enter the rainforests do not have pure motives. Timber from the soaring hardwood trees that dominate many rainforests is in high demand around the world. Woods, such as mahogany and teak, are exported from South American rainforests to industrialized countries. The woods are used to make furniture, flooring, and luxury items for people's homes. Wood is also exported as inexpensive plywood from Southeast Asian rainforests. Unfortunately, the logging practices used to obtain these woods cause damage to the entire forest.

Part of the problem has to do with the structure of most rainforests. Trees of the same species are not clustered closely together, they are mixed in among other trees. If a logging company wants to get a certain type of tree, they will clear-cut an entire section of the forest. They take only the trees they want, leaving the rest lying dead on the ground.

▼ *Good ecotourism companies do not let tourists disturb the forests they are visiting.*

◄ When logging companies cut roads into the forest, other illegal loggers use it to get into the forest and cut down more trees.

NO TREES, POOR SOIL

Once the trees are gone, farmers often move in to try to cultivate the land. Unfortunately, the soil is nutrient-poor to begin with. If there are no tree roots to hold it in place, the soil can be washed away with the rains. Any nutrients that do remain will not last long without replenishment from trees and plants. Before long, the plot of land becomes unusable.

A SOLUTION?

Some people consider selective logging to be a good solution to this problem. In this case, loggers only cut down the trees they need. An advanced form of this method is called "reduced-impact logging". In this case, loggers plan the shortest and best routes they can take to get the selected trees, and they only take a very small number of trees. These newer logging methods are better at reducing damage to the forest, but they do not eliminate it.

TEARING UP THE GROUND

Loggers use heavy equipment, such as tractors that tear up the land as they travel through the forest. They cut roads into the forest to reach the trees they want to fell. These roads provide access into areas that might have been isolated before. Farmers follow these roads to cleared areas and try to cultivate the land.

When a large tree falls, it takes down the smaller trees around it. The resulting hole in the upper canopy throws the entire ecosystem off balance. More sunlight comes into the forest, drying out the forest floor, and leaving the area vulnerable to forest fires. Rainforest fires move slowly but they can spread over huge areas of land. Even if the fire does not kill a tree straight away, the tree may be mortally wounded by the flames and die soon after the fire moves on.

PRECIOUS CARGO

Many rainforests around the world contain natural resources that are even more valuable – from a financial viewpoint – than timber, exotic animals, and medicinal plants.

Minerals and precious gems found in the Amazon basin include diamonds, iron, copper, and gold. French Guiana, which is also in South America, lies in an area known as a "greenstone" belt. This rock formation, which is about two billion years old, is rich in gold deposits. The belt stretches through Venezuela, Guyana, Suriname, Brazil, and French Guiana.

Sierra Leone, which is a country located in Africa, contains rich diamond deposits. Africa is also home to the Congo, which has some of the richest mineral deposits in the world, including diamonds, gold, and uranium. Uranium is a heavy metal that is used in nuclear technology. Nuclear fuel, such as uranium, is used in nuclear power stations to make electricity. It can also be used in dangerous nuclear weapons. Not surprisingly, the wealth found beneath the rainforest floor has brought another type of explorer to the rainforests – miners, hoping to strike it rich.

▼ *Small-scale gold miners use hoses to look for gold in the rainforest near El Dorado in Venezuela.*

GOLD RUSH

In early 2007, El Dorado do Juma became the scene of Brazil's biggest gold rush in more than 20 years. Local people had been quietly mining in this area for years. However, after a local teacher named Ivani Valentin da Silva posted their pictures – and stories of the gold they found – on the Internet, outsiders rushed in. In just two months, an estimated 10,000 people descended on the site. Now, what was once a pristine forest has been turned into a treeless pit, covered with mines and a shanty town made of tree branches and tarpaulin.

PATH OF DESTRUCTION

When large-scale mining companies enter the rainforest, they use many of the same destructive techniques that big logging companies do. These companies clear large sections of forest, and build roads leading to remote areas. Once this path has been cleared into the forest, small-scale miners follow.

Small-scale miners also damage the rainforests. They cut down trees for shelter and for fire, they hunt animals for food, and they use explosives to "dig" for treasure. This loss of tree cover and destruction of riverbanks can lead to erosion and flooding. Also, small-scale miners may not be as careful with the chemicals they use for mining, and some dump their waste into rivers.

▲ This iron mine is in the Amazon rainforest. It is the largest iron mine in the world.

These outsiders may also bring diseases to local tribes in the area. Back in the 18th century, when Spanish explorers arrived in South America they brought diseases that wiped out many tribes. These problems exist today, too. One survey showed that half of all of Brazil's Yanomami tribe suffered from malaria. Malaria was previously unknown to them. Other diseases, such as tuberculosis and hepatitis, are also killing many tribespeople.

TOXIC WASTE

Toxic chemicals are often used in gold mining. Mercury is a poisonous metal. It is used to mine for gold because it makes flakes of gold stick together. This makes the gold easier to gather. Miners are usually careful with mercury, removing most of it, or burning off the excess.

However, sometimes mercury can end up in the rivers. Once the fish are contaminated with mercury, the effects are felt all the way up the **food chain**. Every animal that eats the fish, including humans, will be contaminated.

DEATH BY CYANIDE

Cyanide is a highly toxic chemical that is used to separate gold from surrounding rocks or soil. If cyanide is spilled, as happened in Guyana in August 1995, it can poison the entire surrounding area. Wildlife is killed, the ground is poisoned, and the water becomes undrinkable.

SAVE THE RAINFORESTS!

The world's rainforests are in danger. Every minute, more than 121,000 square (sq m) (145,000 square yards [sq yd]) of rainforest are lost. That is the equivalent of one football pitch every two seconds! This **deforestation** is a result of commercial farming, commercial logging, slash-and-burn farming practices, and the building of roads. This loss threatens the people and animals that call these regions home, and it also threatens the very survival of our planet.

TROUBLE AT HOME

The effects of deforestation are easiest to see at a local level. The loss of trees affects everything else in the area. Without the trees' root systems to hold it in place, soil begins to erode and washes into the rivers. As the soil builds up in rivers and lakes, an area's supply of clean water is compromised. The fish that local people rely on for food may also be affected. Soil holds on to water when it rains. Without the soil and tree roots to hold in water, excessive rain could lead to local flooding.

Loss of habitat also leads to a decline in animals that live in the forest. This impacts local hunters who rely on these animals for food. Worse, loss of habitat could lead to the **extinction** of rainforest species that cannot be found anywhere else on Earth.

▼ Houses on a river's edge must be built on stilts to stay dry during the floods that come during the Amazon's wet season. Deforestation may make flooding much worse.

▶ Golden lion tamarins (Leontopithecus rosali) live in isolated parts of the eastern Atlantic Brazilian rainforest. They are an endangered species as a result of poaching and deforestation.

LOSS OF RESOURCES

Deforestation also takes away a local community's reusable resources. Many things that are supplied by the rainforest, such as fruit, nuts, seeds, oils, and medicinal plants, can be carefully harvested so that they are available year after year. These products are used by local people, but are also important for trade with industrialized nations. Once the trees are gone, these products are gone with them.

Adventure tours are a good way for developing nations to profit from their natural resources without destroying them. Without the forests, there can be no ecotourism business.

GLOBAL IMPACT

Deforestation has far-reaching effects, as well. Rainforests have a big effect on the Earth's climate. During the process of photosynthesis, rainforest trees and plants give off oxygen and take in carbon dioxide from the atmosphere.

Carbon dioxide is a **greenhouse gas**. Greenhouse gases help trap the heat of the Sun within Earth's atmosphere. Trees use carbon dioxide as food and store it in their biomass – their trunk, leaves, roots, and branches. Without trees, too much carbon dioxide would remain in Earth's atmosphere, more heat would be trapped, and the global temperature would rise.

▲ Bananas are just one popular food that originated in the rainforest. Others include chocolate, Brazil nuts, and many spices such as pepper, cinnamon, vanilla, turmeric, and paprika.

CLIMATE CHANGE

As the amount of carbon dioxide in the atmosphere increases, Earth's temperature will rise. This could have a devastating impact on us and our planet. The polar ice caps will melt, and sea levels may rise. This could flood massive areas of land. Our whole climate could change resulting in more frequent and super-strong hurricanes, tornadoes, and other violent weather events.

FINDING SOLUTIONS

We cannot expect only the countries that contain rainforests to work on conservation. These countries are often poor, developing nations that cannot handle alone the **economic** commitment that is needed if we are to conserve a large amount of the world's rainforests. It is up to the global community – every nation in the world – to save Earth's rainforests.

THE KYOTO PROTOCOL

The Kyoto Protocol was first negotiated in 1997 and was fully agreed upon in 2005. The Kyoto Protocol is an international agreement in which more than 160 countries have agreed to dramatically reduce their greenhouse gas emissions by the year 2012. Some countries, including the United States, did not want to sign the agreement. They were worried that the agreement would hurt their economies.

Now, these nations are trying to get approval for another plan that is currently not allowed under the Kyoto Protocol. With this plan, these countries would pay rainforest countries to protect their forests. For example, the United States would pay Brazil to prevent a certain number of rainforest hectares from being destroyed. According to this plan, that would give the United States "credits". It would mean that they would not have to reduce their greenhouse emissions by as much as dictated by the Kyoto agreement.

Some environmentalists are not happy with this plan. They do not like the idea that some countries might try to use the plan to avoid reducing greenhouse emissions. Ideally, rich nations would do both: reduce greenhouse emissions from the burning of **fossil fuels**, such as oil and coal, in industry and transport, and help other nations conserve their rainforests.

▼ Earth is a bright blue jewel in the cold, vast darkness of space. Human influence is hurting the delicate balance of the planet's ecosystem and could eventually lead to the end of life on Earth as we know it.

TOURISM

Ecotourism can also help protect the rainforests. If people are willing to pay to visit the canopies of the Costa Rican rainforest or to see the orang-utans in Borneo, it is worth it for those countries to set aside protected areas called reserves. When a government creates a reserve, people are not allowed to hunt, fish, or cut down trees in that area.

SUSTAINABLE PRACTICES

Introducing sustainable harvesting in these areas can also help with conservation. If local people can earn money from gathering and exporting fruit, seeds, nuts, oils, and medicinal plants, they will be more likely to want to stop deforestation. In addition, sustainable logging practices may help to reduce more destructive, illegal logging practices.

The rainforests are home to some of the most incredible plants and animals in the world. Many cannot be found anywhere else on Earth. And thousands, perhaps millions, still remain to be discovered. These forests, some of the last frontiers on Earth, also play a vital role in maintaining the delicate balance of our planet and sustaining life on Earth. Saving the rainforests seems like a big job, and it is, but every single person who gets involved can make a difference. You do not have to be a scientist or an explorer to help save the rainforests, getting involved on any level can help.

▲ *The first Forest-Stewardship Council (FSC) certified timber company can be found deep in the rainforests of the Congo. This company sells timber that has been harvested using sustainable logging practices.*

WHO'S WHO

There are many organizations around the world dedicated to saving the rainforests, including:

Rainforest Action Network
www.ran.org

Rainforest Alliance
www.rainforest-alliance.org

Wildlife Conservation Society
www.wcs.org

Conservation International
www.conservation.org

FACTS AND STATISTICS

RAINFOREST WEATHER

- Rainforests receive more than 2 m (6.5 ft) of rain every year.
- Temperatures in tropical rainforests range from 21 to 29°C (70 to 85°F).

RAINFOREST DESTRUCTION

- The rainforests are being destroyed at a rate of more than 404,700 sq m (484,000 sq yd) per minute.
- Between 1960 and 1980, Asia lost almost one-third of its rainforests.
- Almost 90 percent of the rainforests on Madagascar have been destroyed.
- Three-quarters of Australia's tropical rainforests have been cleared since the 18th century.
- Almost 65 percent of Central America's rainforests have been cleared and converted to pasture land for cattle.
- As of 2007, only four percent of the world's rainforests are protected.

RAINFOREST BIODIVERSITY

- Rainforests only cover about 6 percent of Earth's surface, but are home to more than 50 percent of all the world's known species of plants and animals.
- One-third of all the birds in the world live in rainforests.
- There are 30,000 species of epiphyte in the rainforests.
- The upper canopy is home to 90 percent of rainforest inhabitants.
- Rainforest trees rely on birds, insects, and other animals, instead of wind, for seed dispersal.
- Most of a rainforest's nutrients are stored in plants, rather than in the soil.

FOOD PRODUCTS

These food products all originated in the rainforests:

- Avocados
- Bananas
- Brazil nuts
- Cashews
- Chocolate
- Coconuts
- Coffee
- Corn
- Figs
- Grapefruit
- Guavas
- Lemons
- Mangos
- Oranges
- Pineapples
- Rice
- Spices, such as black pepper, cayenne, and ginger
- Sugar
- Tomatoes
- Potatoes
- Yams
- Vanilla

RAINFORESTS AROUND THE WORLD

This list includes some of the main rainforests of the world. The size of the rainforests decreases with time as trees are cut down.

AFRICA

Angola
591,000 sq km
(228,200 sq miles)
47.4 percent of total land area

Côte d'Ivoire
104,100 sq km
(40,170 sq miles)
32.7 percent of total land area

Cameroon
212,500 sq km
(82,030 sq miles)
45.6 percent of total land area

Central African Republic
227,600 sq km
(87,860 sq miles)
36.5 percent of total land area

Congo
224,700 sq km
(86,760 sq miles)
65.8 percent of total land area

Democratic Republic of the Congo
1,336,000 sq km
(515,900 sq miles)
58.9 percent of total land area

Equatorial Guinea
16,320 sq km (6,301 sq miles)
58.2 percent of total land area

Gabon
217,800 sq km
(84,070 sq miles)
84.5 percent of total land area

Guinea
67,240 sq km
(25,960 sq miles)
27.4 percent of total land area

Guinea-Bissau
20,720 sq km (8,000 sq miles)
73.7 percent of total land area

Liberia
31,540 sq km
(12,180 sq miles)
32.7 percent of total land area

Madagascar
128,400 sq km
(49,570 sq miles)
22.1 percent of total land area

Malawi
34,020 sq km
(13,140 sq miles)
36.2 percent of total land area

Senegal
86,730 sq km
(33,490 sq miles)
45 percent of total land area

Sierra Leone
27,540 sq km
(10,630 sq miles)
38.5 percent of total land area

Tanzania
352,570 sq km
(136,128 sq miles)
39.9 percent of total land area

Uganda
36,270 sq km
(14,000 sq miles)
18.4 percent of total land area

Zambia
424,520 sq km
(163,900 sq miles)
57.1 percent of total land area

Zimbabwe
175,400 sq km
(67,720 sq miles)
45.3 percent of total land area

SOUTHEAST ASIA

China
1,972,900 sq km
(761,740 sq miles)
21.2 percent of total land area

India
677,010 sq km
(261,390 sq miles)
22.8 percent of total land area

Indonesia
884,950 sq km
(341,680 sq miles)
48.8 percent of total land area

Malaysia
208,900 sq km
(80,660 sq miles)
63.6 percent of total land area

Nepal
36,360 sq km
(14,040 sq miles)
25.4 percent of total land area

Solomon Islands
21,720 sq km (8,386 sq miles)
77.6 percent of total land area

Philippines
71,620 sq km
(27,652 sq miles)
24 percent of total land area

Papua New Guinea
294,370 sq km
(113,660 sq miles)
65 percent of total land area

CENTRAL & SOUTH AMERICA

Brazil
4,776,980 sq km
(1,844,400 sq miles)
57.2 percent of total
land area

Colombia
607,280 sq km
(234,470 sq miles)
58.5 percent of total
land area

Ecuador
108,530 sq km
(41,903 sq miles)
39.2 percent of total
land area

French Guiana
80,630 sq km
(31,131 sq miles)
91.8 percent of total
land area

Guyana
54,374 sq km
(20,990 sq miles)
27.6 percent of total
land area

Nicaragua
51,890 sq km
(20,035 sq miles)
42.7 percent of total
land area

Paraguay
184,750 sq km
(71,332 sq miles)
46.5 percent of total
land area

Peru
687,420 sq km
(265,415 sq miles)
53.7 percent of total
land area

Suriname
147,760 sq km
(57,050 sq miles)
94.7 percent of total
land area

Venezuela
477,130 sq km
(184,220 sq miles)
54.1 percent of total
land area

THE TOP TEN MOST BIODIVERSE COUNTRIES

1. Brazil
2. Colombia
3. Indonesia
4. Peru
5. Mexico
6. Ecuador
7. China
8. India
9. Venezuela
10. Australia

FURTHER RESOURCES

BOOKS

Animals Under Threat: Orangutan,
David Orme, Heinemann Library, 2004

*Deep Jungle: Journey to the Heart of the
Rainforest*, Fred Pearce, Eden Books/
Transworld, 2006

Earth Watch: Saving the Rainforest,
Sally Morgan, Franklin Watts, 2005

Geography Focus: Changing Climate,
Louise Spilsbury, Raintree, 2006

Green Alert: Vanishing Forests, Cheng Puay
Lim, Raintree, 2004

Kingfisher Voyages: Rainforest, Jinny Johnson
and Nalini Nadkarni, Kingfisher Books, 2006

Rainforest Revealed, Jen Green, Dorling
Kindersley, 2004

*Remarkable Rainforest: An Active-Learning
Book for Kids*, Toni Albert, Trickle Creek
Books, 2003

The Amazon Rainforest, Bernard Smith,
Longman, 2005

WEBSITES

**http://earthobservatory.nasa.gov/
Laboratory/Biome/biorainforest.html**
Visit NASA's Earth observatory page to learn
more about rainforests around the world.

**http://passporttoknowledge.com/
rainforest/main.html**
Explore the world's largest rainforest with
researchers who share their field journals,
photos, and more.

www.rainforestconcern.org
Visit the Kids Page on this site to take a guided
tour of the rainforest, try to solve rainforest
riddles, and take a fun animal quiz.

www.rainforest.org
This site is run by the Tropical Rainforest
Coalition (TRC), which works to protect
rainforests and indigenous forest people. Visit
the site for information on how you can help.

www.rainforestlive.org.uk
Explore the rainforest at Rainforest Live. This
site includes a Kidz Korner, where you can
colour, play games, and even enter contests.

www.rainforestweb.org
This site, the world's rainforest information
portal, provides links to sites about indigenous
people of the rainforests, the animals that live
there, rainforest conservation, and more.

GLOSSARY

arboreal something that lives in or spends a lot of time in trees

biodegradable able to be broken down into a harmless substance by living things

biodiversity number of different plants and animals that inhabit a certain piece of land

cannibal human who eats human flesh

climate average weather conditions in an area over a long period of time

conservationist person who fights for the protection of natural resources

conserve protect or keep safe

decompose break down or rot

deforestation removal of trees in a forest to provide land for agricultural purposes, buildings, roads, or to use the trees for building materials or fuel

dirigible self-propelled airship or gas-filled balloon

diverse collection of many different things

ecology study of how living things interact with each other and their environment

economic to do with the production, distribution, and consumption of goods and services

ecosystem small or large part of the environment containing a community of plant and animal life

ecotourism tourism directed towards unspoilt natural environments and intended to support conservation efforts

elevation measure of how far something is above sea level

encroach move into someone else's land

endemic native to a particular place

epiphyte plant that grows on another plant but does not take any nourishment from it

evergreen plant with foliage that remains green throughout the year

evolution how a living thing changes gradually over a very long period of time

exotic unusual

extinction when a certain species is no longer in existence

food chain arrangement of organisms in an ecosystem where one member preys on the member below it on the chain

fossil fuel fuel, such as gas, oil, or coal, that is formed in the Earth from the remains of plants or animals

greenhouse gas gas, such as carbon dioxide, that traps heat inside Earth's atmosphere

habitat natural home for a plant or animal

humidity water content in the air

ice age period during which a large part of Earth's surface was covered with ice and snow

indigenous people that originated in the place where they currently live

influence have an effect on something

infrared heat energy that cannot be seen by humans without special equipment

isolated alone or unique

microbe tiny organism, such as bacteria, that can only be seen under a microscope

mineral substance obtained by mining

missionary someone who tries to convert other people to a certain religion

naturalist person who studies nature, specifically plants or animals

nutrient chemical compounds that make up food

obstacle something that gets in the way of progress

organism living thing

oxbow u-shaped bend in a river

photosynthesis process in green plants in which carbon dioxide, water, and sunlight are used to create food for the plant, and oxygen is released into the air

poaching killing animals illegally

pollination transferring pollen from the male part of a plant to the female part for reproductive purposes

pollution man-made waste that is disposed of in a natural environment

predator animal that hunts, kills, and eats other animals

primate mammal that has well-developed hands for grasping: includes monkeys, apes, humans, and lemurs

remote distant, out of the way, or secluded

river basin land surrounding a river

sapling young tree

specimen part of a group (such as a plant or animal species) that is taken for study

symbiotic when individuals of one species provide those of another with resources, and both individuals benefit

temperate area with moderate temperatures

toxic something poisonous that can kill a person or make them very sick

tributary small stream that feeds into a larger stream or river

understorey vegetation found in the layer beneath the upper canopy but above the forest floor

upper canopy spreading branches of the topmost layer of a forest

vegetation plant life

venomous animal that produces a toxin that is harmful to other living creatures

INDEX